Contents

Introduction

Most of us accept that we, and to a lesser extent nature, have caused damage to the natural environment, and in turn to ourselves. The speed at which we have changed our world, especially during the 20th century, made it difficult to understand and control what we were doing to the environment and the effect it was having on our health and that of animals and plants. It is only in the past 50 years or so that most of us have become aware of what has been happening, and only more recently that we have been seriously trying to do something to stop the damage going on and to find a way of limiting it in the future. This book looks at the problems we have created and at some of the solutions we have devised to overcome them. It also looks at the sort of things we can do to make sure the future is a cleaner and healthier one for us and the environment.

Our impact on the environment

Sit back, and just think about how much you rely on the natural environment. The air you breathe, the water you need for drinking, cooking and washing, the soil for growing the food you eat, the land your home stands on – these are some examples of how much you depend on the environment for your most basic needs. Even though we humans need the environment so much, we have a history of destroying and damaging it. The results of this are now affecting us.

Cultivation

Once human beings moved from being hunters and gatherers to being farmers, they started making a serious impact on the Earth's environment. The human population was growing rapidly and people were organizing themselves to live together in larger groups. More land and more food were needed by these groups. The natural sources of food were scarce and the groups were forced to grow and rear their own food. This involved clearing forests to plant their crops and graze their animals. As the practice continued over time most of the forests in certain parts of the world, particularly in Europe, disappeared. The forests of the world are still disappearing today. Small-scale farmers, big ranchers and tobacco growers for example are stripping out huge areas of the Amazonian **rainforests**. Removing rainforest cover from the land exposes the soil to problems like erosion and **leaching** of **nutrients**, and forever destroys the habitats of animals, plants and **indigenous** people.

4

The ENVIRONMENT & You

Alexander Gray

Heinemann
LIBRARY

H www.heinemann.co.uk
Visit our website to find out more information about **Heinemann Library** books.

To order:
☎ Phone 44 (0) 1865 888066
▤ Send a fax to 44 (0) 1865 314091
▭ Visit the Heinemann Bookshop at www.heinemann.co.uk to browse our catalogue and order online.

First published in Great Britain by Heinemann Library, Halley Court, Jordan Hill, Oxford OX2 8EJ, a division of Reed Educational and Professional Publishing Ltd. Heinemann is a registered trademark of Reed Educational & Professional Publishing Limited.

OXFORD MELBOURNE AUCKLAND JOHANNESBURG BLANTYRE
GABORONE IBADAN PORTSMOUTH NH (USA) CHICAGO

Designed by Tinstar Design (www.tinstar.co.uk)
Originated by Ambassador Litho Ltd
Printed in Hong Kong/China

ISBN 0 431 03541 5   (hardback)
04 03 02 01
10 9 8 7 6 5 4 3 2 1

ISBN 0 431 03548 2   (paperback)
05 04 03 02 01
10 9 8 7 6 5 4 3 2 1

British Library Cataloguing in Publication Data
Gray, Alexander
      The environment and you. – (What's at issue?)
      1. Ecology – Juvenile literature 2. Environmental ethics – Juvenile literature
      I. Title
      333.7

Acknowledgements
The publishers would like to thank the following for permission to reproduce photographs:
Corbis: Hulton Deutsch p20, David H Wells p27, Galen Rowell p37; Ecoscene: Pat Groves p6, Judith Platt p14, Wayne Lawler p23, Sally Morgan p35, Rod Gill p36; Environmental Images: Graham Burns p4, Herbert Giradet p7, Martin Bond p9, Toby Adamson p26, Erini Rodis 31; NASA/Science Photo Library: p11; Greenpeace: Hodson pp12, 13; NHPA: Anthony Bannister p33; Reed pp42, 43; Rex Features: p39, Sipa Press pp28, 40, 41; Science Photo Library: NOAA p10; Tony Stone Images: David Woodfall pp16, 19, David Frazier p20, Ed Pritchard p25.

Cover photograph: Ecoscene: Erik Schaffer

Our thanks to Julie Turner (School Counsellor, Banbury School, Oxfordshire) for her comments in the preparation of this book.

Any words appearing in the text in bold, **like this**, are explained in the Glossary.

Industrialization

In the past 200 years or so, urbanization and industrialization in the world have damaged the environment more than anything else in the Earth's history. Vast manufacturing industries were founded on technological know-how and natural resources such as coal, iron and cotton. Great industrial cities grew and people flocked to them from the countryside to find jobs and housing. Such concentrations of people and industries had a huge effect on the environment – polluting the air, land and water and destroying wildlife habitats.

The dumping of poisonous waste from industry, households and mining operations has polluted oceans, rivers, lakes and **groundwater**. In some parts of the world water has become so contaminated that fish and plants cannot live in it. Toxic wastes from chemical and nuclear works have so badly spoiled the land that it's dangerous for humans and wildlife to live on it.

Progress or just change?

Pressures on the environment mounted during the 20th century. The world's population was expanding faster than ever, creating greater demands for food, consumer goods, energy, houses, roads. The growth of cities, industries, farming, and power generation is still seriously damaging the environment, making it more unhealthy for the humans, animals and plants living in it. **Fossil-fuel** pollution from the burning of coal in factories, power stations and households has contaminated the air and **slag heaps** of waste from mining have disfigured landscapes. The use of petrol to power motor vehicles and aircraft have added substantially to pollution of the air. Gases given off by fossil-fuel have contributed to **global warming** and acid rain and the use of **CFCs** in making products such as refrigerators is said to have contributed to the depletion (thinning) of the **ozone** layer in the atmosphere.

The effects of industrialization – pollution from a petro-chemical complex in Scotland.

CHANGING ATTITUDES

Fortunately we now recognize the damage humans have done and the need to do something about it.

- We are now using less polluting fuels and are turning to renewable sources of energy.

- We are using cleaner petrol for powering cars and are encouraging more people to use public transport.

- We have banned ozone-depleting chemicals from manufacturing.

- We are cleaning up polluted land and managing **landfill** sites a lot better so as to reduce leaking of poisonous waste.

- We have banned the dumping of toxic wastes and **sewage** in oceans and rivers and have passed laws to make polluters pay for cleaning up.

- We have reached agreement with other nations to protect the environment.

- We have created national parks, sites of scientific interest, green belts, etc. to protect designated areas.

Polluting the air

If you live in a city or in the countryside near a motorway you only have to look up to see the rust-coloured haze of **pollution** in the sky. You know from the media and from what you can see for yourself that air pollution is a serious problem. So what is it, how is it caused and how does it affect you?

Air pollution is caused by people and nature. They act in ways that give off gases, smoke, soot and dust that rise into the air and change the natural balance of the atmosphere, making it worse. In turn, the air you and other living things breathe is poorer, and this can damage your health and threaten the survival of animals and plants.

People and nature

People are the worst polluters of the air they breathe. They do this by driving motor vehicles, flying aeroplanes, burning forests, making chemicals, refining oil, producing electricity, and so on. Nature plays a much smaller part in polluting the air. The worst offenders are volcanoes, which erupt gas and ash, and dust storms, which whip loose soil up into the air.

The effects of air pollution
Smog and health

Big cities and areas of heavy industry have the worst **smog** as heavily polluted areas are the most affected. You can see from the traffic jams in a big city like London the amount of fumes being discharged into the air from car exhausts. If you live near a factory you can see the smoke pouring out of its chimney stacks every day. Smog causes respiratory problems, such as bronchitis, lung diseases, eye and

Cyclists in big cities often wear masks so that they don't breathe in exhaust fumes from cars.

Damage from pollution and acid rain has killed off these spruce trees.

lung irritation, headaches and fatigue. Air pollution may aggravate asthma or trigger an attack.

Damage to the environment

Some of the gases given off by car exhausts return to Earth as acid rain. This can seriously damage the environment. You may live in an area where the lakes and rivers have become so affected by acid rain that anything living in them will die, or where the fertility of soil has been so damaged that plants have difficulty growing. Huge parts of the northern hemisphere's forests have actually been destroyed by acid rain. In cities you can see the damage it causes from the pitted stonework and the discolouration (to a dark colour) of buildings.

Warming the world

You probably know that air pollution may be making the world warmer. This is sometimes called **global warming**. It happens because the balance of **greenhouse gases**, which maintain the temperature of the Earth, has been upset by pollution and this has caused the Earth's temperature to rise. The worry is that this may cause mountain glaciers and ice sheets in the Arctic and Antarctica to melt and the seas to rise, causing low-lying parts of the world to flood. In Britain this would affect low-lying areas such as Norfolk.

FACTS

● *The health and life of all living things depend on the quality of the air. Pure air is mostly made up of oxygen (78%) and nitrogen (12%), with smaller amounts of other gases, such as carbon dioxide (0.2%).*

● *We are sending more gases into the atmosphere every year. Carbon dioxide (72%) is by far the greatest contributor to greenhouse gases, followed by methane (18%) and then nitrous oxides (10%). We send more carbon dioxide into the air through burning **fossil fuels** (coal, oil and natural gas) than anything else.*

● *Road traffic in Britain produces 20% of the country's carbon dioxide.*

● *It has been estimated that cattle breaking wind contributes about 100 billion tonnes of methane into the air every year! Even more extraordinary is the contribution made by the world's 250,000 billion termites. A recent estimate puts their methane contribution at 5 billion tonnes.*

Making the air cleaner

You may wonder what you can do to help stop the air being polluted and help make it cleaner. You may also want to know what has been done and is being done by others, such as industry and government, to solve the problem.

Reducing the number of cars on the road

We cannot get rid of cars altogether so we have to find ways of using them less often as a way of reducing **pollution**. One way is to encourage those travelling to work in the same direction to share a car with a few others rather than travel separately in their own cars. This has been encouraged in some countries, such as Australia and Britain. Companies could also encourage this by offering employees interest-free loans for season tickets if they use public transport. In Britain the government is now suggesting charging motorists for travelling into city centres such as London. The money raised could be used to invest in a better public transport system that more people will use instead of the car.

Making the car cleaner

Private cars pollute the air more than anything else, and motor vehicles (cars, buses and trucks) are responsible for two-thirds of the **smog** in cities. Steps have already been taken in some countries to reduce and control the amount of air pollution caused by the motor vehicle. In Britain and elsewhere new cars must be fitted with **catalytic converters** to stop the exhausts blowing out soot.

CASE STUDY

One UK city is trialling a system of banning driver-only cars into the city centre along a key road during rush hour. Cars must have at least one passenger. This has already reduced rush-hour delays and improved movement through the city.

Petroleum companies have devised ways of making petrol cleaner. Removing lead from petrol reduces the amount of pollution from cars. You will notice that all petrol stations now have unleaded petrol pumps and this is a growing trend elsewhere. The petroleum companies have also been advertising their concern for green issues, which helps raise people's awareness of the pollution problem.

CLEANER PETROL

Petrol without lead burns more efficiently than leaded petrol and so gives off less carbon dioxide. This is also true if oxygen is added to petrol. Therefore, we can expect less pollution from petrol containing oxygen and no lead.

Alternative sources of energy

Use of cleaner alternative sources of energy can help improve the condition of the air. Electric cars are used in some city centres to cut down pollution, though the inconvenience of recharging them limits their attractions for the moment. Natural gas is cleaner than petrol and in some parts of the world is being used in motor vehicles.

Cutting industrial pollution

Many industries still use **fossil fuels**, especially coal, to generate power. But new ways have been devised to reduce the amount of pollution caused by these industries. It is now possible to reduce the amount of sulphur dioxide, one of the acid rain gases, given off by coal-fired electricity power stations.

International cooperation

Warnings from scientists, environmentalists, national and local protest groups and individual governments themselves increased the pressure on nations to cooperate in solving the problem of air pollution. This led to various agreements as to how to do this. At the 1982 Stockholm Conference 35 countries agreed to cut acid rain by reducing their **emissions** of sulphur by 30 per cent in 10 years. In 1987 the major industrialized nations agreed to reduce the production and use of five of the most harmful gases used in aerosol sprays, refrigerators, **solvents** and plastic foam. At the 1992 United Nations Summit in Rio de Janeiro in Brazil 160 countries signed an agreement to reduce the emission of **greenhouse gases**.

FACT

- *In Britain only 1 in 50 journeys are made by bicycle, whereas in Holland it is nearly 1 in 3.*

You can help to reduce air pollution by walking, or for longer journeys, travelling by tram or other methods of public transport.

WHAT YOU CAN DO

- You can walk or cycle to school, to the shops, to visit friends, to the sports field. For longer journeys you can take the bus, the train, a tram, the underground.

- You can try to persuade car owners to buy smaller cars that use less petrol, take up less space on the road and give off less pollution.

- You can join an environmental group that exerts pressure on the government and companies to take whatever action is needed to stop pollution.

- You can take part in local protests against pollution and help with fund-raising.

- You can report any special pollution problems in your area to the government's air pollution service (0800 556677).

The hole in the ozone

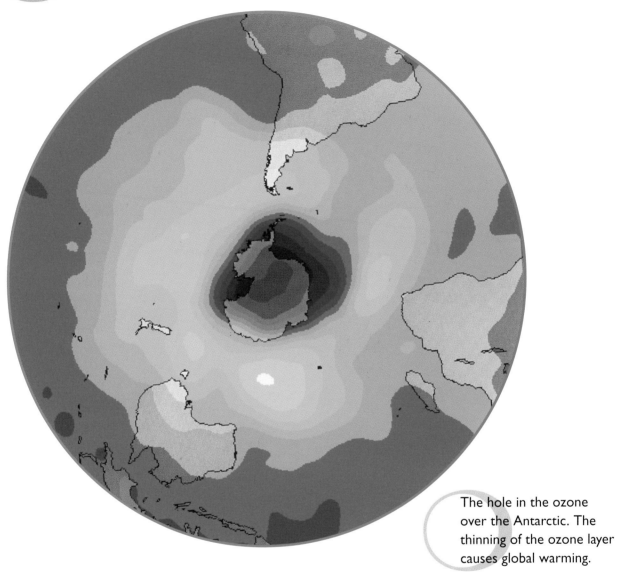

The hole in the ozone over the Antarctic. The thinning of the ozone layer causes global warming.

We are protected from the Sun's harmful **ultraviolet** rays by a layer of gases in the atmosphere – the **ozone layer**. Without this layer our skin would burn and we would suffer serious illnesses such as cancer. The worry is that the ozone layer is thinning out and a 'hole' has formed through which more of the Sun's rays are reaching the Earth. So, why has this happened and what do you have to worry about?

Cause of the hole

Part of the answer to ozone layer thinning is in your own house. Your refrigerators, aerosol sprays and the fire extinguisher, if you have one, use chemicals called **chlorofluorocarbons** (CFCs) and halons. These are the chief culprits in the thinning of the ozone layer. Another is the farmer you see spraying his land to kill pests. He may be using a chemical called methyl bromide, which can seriously damage the ozone layer, as well as causing us serious health problems.

The problem with these chemicals is that when they pass into the air they stay there for a long time without naturally breaking down. In that time they move up into the ozone layer. Here they are broken down by the Sun's radiation into chlorine. The chlorine then acts on the ozone, changing it into oxygen.

The effect on people's health

It is calculated that a 1 per cent loss of ozone amounts to roughly a 2 per cent increase in damage to our health. On this basis it is estimated that millions of us will die from cancer by 2075. We could also suffer from eye cataracts and if someone inhaled (breathed in) methyl bromide they could suffer from lung diseases.

The effect on the environment

If the ozone layer thins out the Earth's climate will get increasingly warmer. And if this happens certain changes could take place. Mountain glaciers and the polar ice sheets could melt causing the seas to rise and submerge (cover) some of the low-lying land of the planet. Humans and animals might then have to migrate inland and plants might have to re-adapt to the changes or die.

OZONE IN THE LOWER ATMOSPHERE

Ozone can also build up in the lower layers of the atmosphere. This is due to the amount of **fossil fuel** gases that are emitted into the air from motor vehicles and industry. It's a serious problem in some major cities, such as Los Angeles, where the combination of gases, sunlight and the surrounding mountains has resulted in a serious build up of ozone above the city. This can affect the health of people, causing respiratory problems and eye irritation and it can poison trees, plants and crops. It can also affect the climate and contribute to **global warming**.

FACT

● *Ozone is a gas, a form of oxygen, present throughout the atmosphere. 90% of it forms a layer of gas in the upper atmosphere, about 20 kilometres above the Earth's surface. It protects us and the environment by stopping 97% of the Sun's harmful ultraviolet rays reaching the Earth.*

Scientists studying an ozone concentration print-out.

Filling the hole

You may be sufficiently worried about the **ozone layer** to want to do something about it. Some things have already been done by governments, environmentalists and individuals. Many governments have already banned the use of chemicals that were destroying the ozone layer. Environmentalists campaigned against **CFCs** and pressurised governments, companies and individuals to ban or refrain from using those chemicals that damage the ozone.

Environmentalist pressure

Chemical companies in Britain and Europe opposed the banning of CFCs. They influenced governments not to ban them. It took the action of environmental groups to increase the pressure on companies and governments to do something about the chemicals and to make the public aware of the problem and get their help.

In Britain the environmentalist group Friends of the Earth campaigned to make people aware of the effect the chemicals were having. In 1986 the group published a listing of aerosols ('The Aerosol Connection') that did not use CFCs and called on the public to buy these instead of the ones with CFCs. The press got involved and covered the campaign. Soon thousands were asking for the information.

Environmental groups organize protests to encourage governments and big companies to improve their policies on environmental issues.

At this time McDonald's fast-food outlets were using cartons made of CFC foam to hold their hamburgers. Friends of the Earth called on the public to hand these back to the company as a gesture of opposition to their use. The huge media coverage of the gesture forced McDonald's to change to a non-CFC foam carton.

The fast-growing public opposition to CFCs forced the chemical companies of Europe on to the back-foot and compelled governments to accept the message to get rid of CFCs. By 1990 the USA and most of Western Europe had agreed to get rid of CFCs and many industrial companies had already decided to stop using them at all.

Getting rid of CFCs

The attack on CFCs really began worldwide in 1985 when the ozone 'hole' was discovered over the Antarctic. The UN declared that controlling CFCs was then the most important ecological issue. At the Montreal Protocol on the Depletion of the Ozone Layer meeting of industrialized nations in 1987 countries such as Britain, USA, France, Japan and Canada agreed to reduce their use of CFCs by 50 per cent.

The USA took the Montreal agreement further by deciding to end all use of CFCs by 1996. Some of America's giant corporations, such as the DuPont company, took matters into their own hands, and declared their intention to end all use of the chemicals by 1994. The USA also declared it would end the use of methyl bromide by the end of the 20th century.

SUBSTITUTES FOR CFCS

HFCs (hydrofluorocarbons) have been used instead of CFCs. These are less harmful than CFCs as they tend to break down quickly in the atmosphere. The effect they have is more gradual than CFCs. HFCs can be used for refrigeration, in air-conditioning, in foams and for medical aerosols.

The future

It's unlikely that CFCs will suddenly disappear from the atmosphere the moment we stop using them. They have been building up in the atmosphere for many years and will linger for some time. According to the United Nations it will take until 2040 for the ozone layer to get back to normal. The United Nations hopes that the effects of CFCs on the ozone layer will have peaked by 2000.

WHAT YOU CAN DO

- You could persuade your family to try giving up aerosols, such as hair sprays and body sprays, that can be easily substituted by non-aerosol devices.

- Campaign to stop farmers using chemicals for spraying their land and maybe think about eating organically grown food (this could help strengthen demand and make it more viable for farmers to change to **organic** methods of farming).

- Persuade your family to change the refrigerator – and get one without CFCs.

- Help campaign against the use of aerosols altogether.

This banner was displayed on the Houses of Parliament in London as a protest against ozone depleting chemicals.

Acid rain

As you hurry home through the rain or snow it may never occur to you that there is anything more harmful in it than getting wet. But the rain or snow is likely to contain some acid. Normally the amount is too small to have any effect on you. But in special conditions the amount of acid might be large enough to have a damaging effect on people's health, and it could even be fatal. As for the environment the effect of high levels of acid over a period of time can be devastating.

What is acid rain?

Acid rain forms in the atmosphere and falls on the Earth as rain, mist, fog, smog, sleet or snow. It is formed from some of the gases we pollute the atmosphere with. These gases, such as sulphur dioxide and nitrogen oxide, are turned into highly **corrosive** acids by the action of sunlight, oxygen and water. They become part of clouds that form in the atmosphere and when water from the clouds falls to Earth as rain it carries acid with it.

Sources of acid rain

The world's worst polluters are in the northern hemisphere, where most of the industrialized countries are. Power stations and oil refineries are two of the worst culprits. In Britain the power stations at Ferrybridge, Drax and Eggborough in the Aire Valley in Yorkshire send out 600,000 tonnes of sulphur dioxide every year. The gases emitted by cars are another source of acid rain and volcanoes add more to acid rain than any other natural source.

Corrosive acids present in rainwater cause erosion to buildings like on the top of this church in Lincolnshire, UK.

NATURAL SOURCE

When Mt Pinatubo in the Philippines erupted on 15 June 1991 an estimated 30 million tonnes of sulphur dioxide was ejected into the atmosphere. This then fell to Earth as acid rain.

Damage to the environment

Acid rain damages the environment in lots of ways. If it passes down into the ground it will poison the **groundwater** supplies, making it unsuitable for humans to drink. It can make soil too acidic for plants to grow and it can make lakes and rivers too acidic for natural life to survive. In Sweden 20,000 lakes have been poisoned by acid rain and about a fifth of them have lost all their fish. Some of this acid rain has its source in the pollution generated by Yorkshire's power stations.

You only have to look at the pitted and discoloured stonework of some buildings, particularly limestone ones, to see how they have been affected by acid rain. London's St Paul's Cathedral is a good example of a limestone building whose stonework has been corroded and discoloured by acid rain.

Damage to our health

People's health can be damaged through breathing in acidic water droplets from the air.

London's famous five-day 'pea-souper' **smog** in early December 1952 killed 4000 people. They died from breathing in water droplets in the air. The smog was caused by still, warm air trapping a cloud **saturated** in sulphuric acid. If there had been a wind it would have broken up the cloud and blown it away. In high temperatures and still air nitrogen oxide levels in the air may get so great that it is difficult for people to breathe.

Coping with acid rain

Some countries are making efforts to reduce the amount of acid rain by cleaning up emissions from factories, power stations and motor vehicles. Others are switching from heavy polluting energy-producing fuels to cleaner forms of energy, such as hydroelectricity and **solar energy**. Some companies have adopted an environmental approach in parts of their businesses.

Countries have recognized that this is a global problem and have made formal agreements on reducing the amount of acid rain in the atmosphere. The first one was signed in 1979 at the Convention on Long-Range Transboundary Air Pollution. This agreement was the focus for the environmentalists' campaign against acid rain during the following ten years. This was followed by the Conference on the Acidification of the Atmosphere in 1982. In the same year the Thirty Per Cent Club was born, made up of 35 countries who agreed to cut emissions of sulphur by 30 per cent in 10 years.

FACT

● *On 1 October 1991 Athenians sweltered in temperatures of 36°C and struggled to breathe as nitrogen oxide levels in the air soared in the heat. Two hundred people had to be treated in hospital for respiratory and heart problems. The Greek government reacted by banning all private cars from the city in an effort to cut the levels of pollution.*

Poisoning the water

You may enjoy swimming in rivers, lakes or seas. However we need these natural sources of water for drinking and we need to harness the power of rivers for producing hydroelectricity. But we also use our water resources for dumping waste from our households, factories and farms.

Contaminating the rivers

In the wealthier countries we pour vast amounts of household and factory waste into the rivers. The poisonous **nitrates**, heavy metals and oils of factory waste are deadly to wildlife in those rivers. In countries where there is inadequate sewerage and water facilities the rivers and streams are often used as open sewers and as sources of drinking water. This creates serious health hazards for the people and diseases such as cholera and typhoid are common.

Rivers and **groundwater** supplies are also contaminated by fertilizers and pesticides washed into them from farmland and by poisons leaking from **landfill** sites.

Contaminating the lakes

Lakes are sometimes contaminated by detergents and **fertilizer nitrates** from households, factories and farms. These most commonly enter lakes from dumping in rivers and water running-off from fertilised farmland. You may have seen the result of this in the **algae** that forms and spreads on the surface of lakes. This algae blanket blocks out the light that the lake's aquatic plants need to survive. These plants will eventually die and decay. When this happens **bacteria** flourishes and starts to use up more and more of the oxygen of the lake. This will deprive the lake's fish of the oxygen they need to live. Eventually the lake's whole **ecosystem** will collapse.

Contaminating the seas

We use the sea shores for many pleasures. But how often have you been discouraged from the beach by washed-up waste, or from swimming in the sea by seeing an open **sewage** pipe nearby.

Sewage discharge

In Britain more than 300 million gallons of sewage is discharged every day into the sea around the coast. Much of this is untreated. The greatest worry is the effect it has on bathing beaches where millions of people holiday every year. People can get infected with bacteria from the sewage and suffer certain illnesses, such as gastroenteritis and hepatitis. In the 1980s sunworshippers and surfers on Sydney's world-famous Bondi beach could sometimes see the raw sewage drifting off the beach from a sewage discharge outlet nearby. Recent rules and regulations mean that this is unlikely to happen nowadays.

Industrial waste discharge

Poisonous industrial wastes, such as mercury, lead, arsenic, are dumped directly into the sea or carried there by the rivers into which they were originally dumped. In the sea it's possible for the waste to build up into highly toxic (poisonous) concentrations that contaminates the sea life that feeds on it, particularly fish. If contaminated fish is then caught by humans or animals for food the poison enters the **food chains** of these other living things.

Nuclear waste discharge

In Britain the local beaches around the Sellafield **nuclear** power station became so contaminated by nuclear waste that far fewer people now visit the area. People poisoned by **radioactivity** can develop various forms of cancer.

Some of the sewage that is washed into the sea is untreated and bad for people's health.

Oil spillage

Oil spillage is one of the big issues of environmental damage. Major oil spills from oil tankers damaged at sea tend to grab the headlines and anger environmentalists. Most of the 36 million tonnes of oil spilt into the seas each year comes from these accidents. Sea life and resort beaches are often contaminated by the spillage being washed ashore. The loss of wildlife and the cost of cleaning up can be massive.

Contaminating drinking water

Drinking water is sometimes contaminated by too many nitrates seeping into the groundwater supplies from farms using fertilizers. The nitrates can build up to dangerous levels and poison anyone drinking the water. The **World Health Organization** revealed in the 1980s that 'blue baby' (babies that have a lack of oxygen in their blood) births were caused by nitrate poisoning.

FACT

● *1 in 5 of Britain's beaches are said to fall below European standards for acceptable levels of* **bacteria** *in the water.*

Cleaning the water

Our water resources need to be protected and cleaned up to avoid causing more damage to ourselves and the environment. The British government has laid down regulations and imposed bans on the disposal of waste and has set limits on what we introduce into our drinking water to make it safe. Pressure groups have highlighted the behaviour of water polluters, particularly big companies, and forced them to face up to their responsibilities to us and the environment. You can do something yourself to help.

Who protects your water?

In Britain our rivers, **groundwater** and sea waters are protected by the the government's Environment Agency. The Agency has the power to permit or deny anyone the right to dump waste in our rivers and seas. It also has the power to make companies follow the standards of **pollution** that have been officially set. Water companies also have the power to allow or deny industry the right to dispose liquid waste in the **sewage** system.

There's a blue flag scheme in Britain which is designed to help improve the quality of Britain's beaches. A beach that meets the standards set down is awarded a blue flag indicating this. Many local councils work hard to raise the standards of their beaches. Having a blue flag is used in promoting the attractions of an area for visitors.

There are also European standards for beaches, the European Community Bathing Water Directive, which applies to Britain. It particularly relates to the amount of **bacteria** in the water that comes from pollution. So far Anglian Water is the only British water company to actually meet the minimum conditions of the directive for bathing beaches.

Sewage dumping bans

The banning of sewage dumping is another way for governments to control the impact it has on people and the environment. The US government in 1972 banned the dumping of sewage in the oceans around the country; instead **landfill** sites were to be used or the sewage converted from sludge to **fertilizers**. Los Angeles for example stopped dumping in the Pacific in 1987. But many companies and local authorities simply ignored it. In 1992 the ban was reinforced with harsh punishments. Anyone ignoring the ban now risked being fined a million dollars a day. This was enough to persuade some cities who had previously ignored the ban to change their minds.

Sewage treatment

Several areas in Britain are receiving special treatment of sewage to make it safe to discharge it into the sea close to beaches. **Ultraviolet (UV)** disinfection is being used in the treatment works for Porthtowan and Mt Hawke in Wales so that discharges into the stream that cuts across Porthtowan Beach do not contain infectious bacteria. A UV treatment plant has also been established at Aveton Gifford in South Devon to avoid contaminating the shellfish in the local estuary.

Making drinking water safer

In Britain the quality of our drinking water is protected by a European law (the Drinking Water Directive) which sets limits on the amount of pollutants that are allowed in water.

Drinking water can be treated in certain ways to make it safer to drink. The **World Health Organization** recommends limits to the amount of **nitrates** in drinking water. The European Community has done likewise. The trouble is that these limits are often violated.

The nitrates that **run off** farms can be removed from water by using chemicals and the amount of nitrates in fertilizers can be reduced. Aluminium powder can also be used to turn nitrates into less harmful chemicals, such as ammonia.

WHAT YOU CAN DO

Here are various things you can do to help prevent further pollution of the water resources of the country.

- Recycle as much as you can to help reduce the amount of waste dumped in landfill sites, which leak poisons into rivers and groundwater.

- Don't clean your paint brushes in the sink so that you don't flush the paint through the sewage system.

- Do not let your family use **pesticides** for killing pests in the garden. They may be washed into the drains by the rain and pass into the sewage system.

- You could volunteer to help clean up refuse from contaminated areas.

- Buying **organic** food helps strengthen demand and makes it more viable for farmers to change to organic methods of farming.

- If you know your water company is breaking the law report it to the Environment Agency (Emergency hotline 0800 80 70 60).

- If you believe your water company is falling down on its responsibilites to improve water pollution report it to the water regulator's (Ofwat) local branch, your MP, or your local newspaper.

FACT

- *In 1998 the Milford Port Authority was fined £4 million. This was the largest fine in British environmental history. It was imposed for the Authority's responsibility in the grounding of the* Sea Empress *off the Pembrokeshire coast in 1996 and the subsequent pollution of the coastline. This was intended to send out the message to anyone polluting the environment that they would be treated toughly.*

Impact on the land

If you live in a city you cannot help being aware of how it keeps growing outwards, encroaching more and more on the countryside. Congested city centres, the construction of roads, factories, offices and houses are all signs of this. In the countryside you can see how farms are bigger than they used to be, how intensive the farming is, how many chemicals are used to keep the soil fertile and kill pests, how crowded together the animals are, how much bigger the machinery is. These developments exert greater pressures on the natural resources and affect the quality of our lives and the state of the environment.

Since the 1930s cities have grown and become more congested and more polluted.

The city and the environment

The growth and expansion of cities has had a damaging impact on wildlife in the UK. City expansion involves acquiring more land for suburban development, industrial areas and leisure activities, such as golf courses. This means taking over parts of the countryside and squeezing animals and plants out of their habitats. It also increases **pollution** of these areas.

Cities can also increase the risk of natural hazards. A city imposes different surfaces on the land – buildings, roads and pavements. One consequence is that rainwater, which once seeped into the ground when it fell, now flows over the solid surfaces of roads, pavements and buildings. You can see for yourself what happens when it's raining hard. Rainwater gushes along the gutters of streets and roofs down into drains and along the **sewage** system, and into rivers. This raises the volume of water in the rivers and increases the risk of flooding.

Farming and wildlife

Farming in Britain became increasingly more intensive after 1945 to meet the expanding population and greater demands for food, but the environment suffered. The need to cultivate larger areas of land to grow crops on a grander scale has destroyed many wildlife habitats. Britain has lost over 20 per cent of its hedgerows to make way for larger fields.

Many wetland wildlife habitats in this country have also been lost to farming. Bogs, water meadows and marshes have been drained and converted for crop cultivation. Other areas have been polluted by **fertilizers** and drained for irrigation. Many of Britain's wild forests full of native species have also been lost to farming.

Rivers and **groundwater** supplies have been polluted by **intensive farming**. The use of fertilizers and **pesticides**, which are used to keep soils productive and destroy pests, has resulted in **nitrates** seeping into the groundwater (drinking water) and **phosphates running off** into rivers. Intensively rearing animals to produce more food has also led to the contamination of water. Housing huge numbers of hens in battery pens to produce more eggs and keeping large numbers of cattle together in pens for fattening produces huge amounts of **effluent**. Some of this can get washed into nearby water sources by the rain.

CLEARING LAND

In the developing world, where populations are expanding fast, people are moving into forest areas to clear the land for farming to grow more food. Much of this is small-scale, shifting agriculture, but large areas are also being cleared for ranching, tobacco growing and, in countries such as Colombia, illicit (illegal) drug cultivation. The result of this is that animals, plants and **indigenous** peoples lose their habitats. The greatest loss is in Latin America. Here 20 million acres of **rainforest** is being lost each year.

LAND WITHOUT TREES

Without trees to protect the land more rainwater runs off the surface washing away the soil, sometimes carrying it into rivers, which may then flood. On steep hillsides erosion is a serious problem when rains are heavy, as in monsoon areas such as northern India.

Saving the land

Land is a limited resource. And yet we go on using it carelessly. We put more buildings on it, strip it of trees, over-use its soils and expose them to erosion by rain and wind. At the same time, action is being taken to save and protect the land for the future. Special organizations have been created in Britain to make sure cities do not expand too much into the countryside and pressure groups are active in trying to stop developments, such as new roads, destroying special wildlife habitats.

Protecting wildlife

There is a law in Britain to protect wildlife – the Wildlife and Countryside Act. There are also areas designated as of special scientific interest by conservation bodies such as English Nature and Scottish Natural Heritage. However, these measures are not always strong enough to protect wildlife areas from being damaged.

In Britain the Countryside Commission and the National Trust help to look after the state of the countryside to make sure city expansion doesn't damage nearby natural life. Sometimes local environmentalist groups are capable of organizing opposition to plans that involve destruction of wildlife areas, as in the case of the Twyford Downs protest against the proposed bypass around Winchester, which would have destroyed an important local wildlife habitat.

Restricting the city

The more a city grows the more expensive it becomes to run, particularly in providing services such as roads and policing. And if inner cities are allowed to

In countries where trees have often been chopped down for commercial farming people are now replanting trees to offset the damage caused to the land.

decline, more people will move away. To stop this kind of expansion city planners have come up with various solutions.

Old industrial and commercial buildings (e.g. warehouses) close to city centres have been transformed into apartment blocks; this sort of new housing close to city centres is now a policy of many cities. Waste tips and old industrial sites have been cleaned up and landscaped into parks and play areas. **Green belt** land has also been created around cities to stop them expanding too far.

Planting trees

Many countries after years of chopping down trees to make way for farmland, cities and for making furniture and paper are now replanting trees to offset the damage that stripping the land caused. In some countries conifers are planted for commercial use and deciduous trees are planted for shade and to protect the soil and provide wildlife habitats. In Britain the Forestry Commission plants about 35,000 hectares (82,500 acres) of commercial conifers a year. In Kenya the government initiated a national tree-planting campaign in 1971 and the country's Green Belt Movement encouraged people to plant trees in any open space in villages and towns. By the 1990s thousands of green belts of trees had been created and millions of trees planted.

WHAT PRESSURE GROUPS CAN DO

- Use pressure to stop traffic going through certain wildlife areas and support the reduction of traffic.

- Encourage local community action against development that will destroy habitats.

- Apply pressure to government to strengthen the law to protect wildlife habitats, as the Wildlife and Countryside Link is doing (this is an alliance of environmental and conservation groups).

WHAT FARMERS CAN DO

- Use less **fertilizers** and **pesticides** and so cause less harm to fertile soil and drinking water supplies.

- Engage in **organic** farming as a way of avoiding having to fertilize the lands with artificial chemicals.

- Cut down on water (and so salt contamination of farmland) by using the right amount for the type of soil and for the time of year – some soils and certain seasons don't need as much water as others.

WHAT YOU CAN DO

- Support your local wildlife group, which aims to save, restore and protect the environment. You could become a member and can volunteer to help restore damaged wildlife habitats, such as traditional stone walls. Encourage your family and friends to become members too.

- Join a national environmental or conservation group.

- Report any threats to special wildlife sites to the appropriate environmental or conservation group.

- Persuade your family to eat organically grown food whenever possible to help increase pressure on farmers to change to organic farming.

Too many people?

You have probably seen photos or TV pictures of people starving and dying in some parts of the world where drought has destroyed harvests. Or it may be pictures of people living in overcrowded inner city shanty slums, suffering from poor sanitation, disease, hunger and crime. These are often the problems caused by too many people depending on limited resources to survive. In the cities it may be that there are not enough jobs and houses for the many people who are drawn to live there. This is not just a problem in the poorer parts of the world, it also affects the rich.

The need for food

The environment in any part of the world may only be capable of supporting a certain number of people. Those who need to grow food to survive will need fertile soil and water for drinking and irrigating their crops. In poorer countries where natural resources such as soil and water are limited and where people are barely surviving, any growth in the numbers of people living there may be too much for the environment to bear. In Somalia in North Africa, where the land is poor and the rainfall unreliable, many people spend their lives constantly on the edge of starvation. Their desperation for food is so great that they can only think of farming the land to grow enough food to meet their immediate needs. If they have no way of keeping the land fertile for future farming the soil will become exhausted and turn to dust. In areas adjoining deserts the land will simply become part of the desert.

In some parts of the world it is not so much that there are too many people, it is more that the land is unequally distributed. In Brazil most of the fertile farming land is owned by relatively few large landowners. Most of the small farmers are forced to survive on the poorer land or to clear areas of the rainforest to grow their crops. The result is that large areas of Brazil's **rainforests** are cleared every year for farming, not just by the small farmers but also by the big ranchers, particularly for grazing beef cattle to supply the ever-expanding fast-food chains of the world.

Pressures on the cities

Rising populations and the migration of people from rural areas exerts huge strains on some of the great cities of the world. In Britain the movement of people from other regions to London and the south-east in search of jobs has increased the pressure on land, transport, health services, housing, and so on.

This can create massive problems for the environment and people living in it. More people means more vehicles on the roads polluting the air with more carbon dioxide. In this country the change is relatively gradual and we have time to adjust and learn to cope. Also we are wealthy enough to provide most of the facilities people need.

However in some parts of the world the speed at which the population increases in a city can have a catastrophic effect on the environment and people's lives. Some cities cannot adjust quickly enough to the rapid increase in demand for facilities like housing, jobs, health services, improved sanitation, transport. They may also lack the regulations that help control the pollution of the environment. If a city cannot cope with the numbers of people it has, then parts of it may collapse into extreme poverty with slum dwellings, crime, poor sanitation, disease.

Pressure on land

The more people there are the more land is needed to build houses, offices, roads, leisure facilities, and so on. The more people there are the more polluted and overcrowded the cities become. In wealthier countries many people are escaping the pressures of living in overcrowded cities by migrating to rural areas and commuting to work in the city.

Some cities have developed and grown on new land: Hong Kong has reclaimed much of the sea around its coast for houses and office blocks; in the USA parts of the Florida **Everglades** have been reclaimed to build houses. One effect of this has been to erase much of the natural environment from the planet. Animals and plants have disappeared from some areas after their habitats were destroyed to accommodate the spread of humans.

The level of pollution in cities rises as the population increases.

Reducing the impact of people

You might wonder how it is possible to stop the world's population growing and what can be done to cope with the impact that densely populated areas have on the environment and ourselves. Some countries are already trying to control their birth rates by encouraging people to have smaller families. Better methods of farming are also being introduced in some countries to make the soil more fertile and productive and not so vulnerable to the effects of drought. In this way the pressure of people for food does not exceed what the land can provide.

Controlling birth rate

The pressures on the environment can be eased by controlling the pace at which population grows. This can be done by controlling the size of families but it might require a radical change in attitude and culture. For centuries in some parts of the world it has been the custom for married couples to have as many children as possible. This was to make sure there was enough children to help work the land for the food the family needed to live. These people needed a lot of convincing to change hundreds of years of tradition.

Programmes were set up by governments to educate people in the use of **birth control** methods and free **contraceptives** were supplied. This has had some success. The **United Nations'** birth control programmes in the 1970s also managed to cut down the number of pregnancies in some poorer countries.

A mural promoting single child families in China.

Encouraging smaller families

Many people in poorer countries are now convinced that having smaller families is good, particularly when it means fewer mouths to feed and more money to spread around. People also realize that improvements in standards of living are enjoyed more by having smaller families. And women with greater access to education realize they can take up careers rather spend most of their lives being mothers and housewives.

Sustaining food supplies

Better farming methods are needed in certain countries vulnerable to natural disaster, especially drought, to grow the food needed to feed people and at the same time sustain the fertility of the soil. The use of **fertilizers**, water for irrigation and mixed crop cultivation are some ways of keeping the land fertile enough to go on growing crops for food.

Attempts have been made internationally to stop overfishing, which depletes the world's supplies of fish and creates a problem for those who depend on it as their main source of food. One was the creation of a 200-mile zone around a country's coastal waters that could only be fished by that country's fishing fleets. An international commission was also set up to manage the world's tuna fisheries. However there have been so many infringements of the rules that the population of tuna has continued to drop. A more successful system of fisheries management has been the one used in Japan. Here the coastal fisheries are controlled by local Fisheries Cooperative Associations.

Governments are pushing the message that smaller families are best.

FACTS

● *The rate that humans are multiplying is easing down. In Europe and America it has virtually stopped. The size of the world's population will eventually level out at about 10 to 14 billion, according to the United Nations. This will happen when the birth and death rates balance out.*
● *In the 1960s Bangladeshi women had an average of 6 children; now it's down to 4. Many people are also marrying later and this helps to keep down the size of families. In Bangladesh the average age a woman got married was 14; today it's 18.*

WHAT YOU CAN DO

● Organize your school to hold a jumble sale or go on sponsored walks to raise money to help people in need.

● Collect money for charities helping people who are starving because the land cannot sustain them in food, e.g. Oxfam and Comic Relief.

● Walk or cycle to school to ease transport pressure in your city.

AGAINST THE GRAIN

In the 1930s the district of Machakos in Kenya, on the edge of the Sahara, was on the verge of becoming desert itself. The capacity of the land to support an ever-growing population was about to collapse. However, its people, the Akamba, changed their habits: they nursed the soil back to life and terraced the land to conserve rainwater and stop erosion. The growth in population didn't put the environment under unsustainable pressure. The increase in the number of people was a valuable asset in restoring, and even improving, the environment.

The nuclear problem

Like many people you may have reservations about an industry that is involved in manufacturing weapons of mass destruction. You might also be worried because of the stories you have seen in the media about **nuclear** power station accidents, such as at Chernobyl in Russia in 1986. There are also other worries. The problem of what to do with nuclear waste still has not been entirely resolved and we now have to worry about new nuclear powers who are unfriendly towards one another – India and Pakistan.

Testing nuclear weapons

In the 1950s and early 1960s Britain, France and the USA tested nuclear weapons in Australia and in the Pacific region. More than 250 tests were carried out during this time. These tests had an effect on the environment of the region and the people who lived there. The tests involved setting off a nuclear explosion on a remote island in the area. The explosion sent masses of **radioactive** dust into the atmosphere. You may be aware of the mushroom cloud of dust that became an abiding image of these tests. The dust was sometimes carried by wind to other areas. From there it showered down on the surrounding land and water and on anything living there. The radioactivity contaminated land, water, animals and people. Some of the people poisoned by it became seriously ill. Thyroid gland disease and bone cancer are two of the worst human diseases caused by radioactive poisoning.

In 1996 the French government carried out its sixth and largest nuclear test in the South Pacific.

Nuclear accidents

Nuclear power station accidents in recent years have badly shaken our confidence in nuclear energy. Chernobyl has been the worst so far. Other high-profile accidents occurred at Sellafield in the north-west of England in 1957 and at Three Mile Island power station near Harrisburg in Pennsylvania in eastern USA in 1979. The latest major accident occurred in Japan in 1999, in a nuclear station not far from Tokyo, the country's most populated city.

Nuclear waste

Nuclear waste is dangerous. It is highly radioactive and poisonous. It includes chemicals left behind by factories making nuclear weapons and spent (used) fuel rods left behind by nuclear power stations producing energy. What to do with the waste has been a problem for some time. The trouble is that some of it takes thousands of years before it breaks down naturally and becomes harmless. There is also a huge amount to get rid of.

Nuclear waste has to be removed from where it is produced and stored somewhere safe. When nuclear weapons manufacturers close down a factory they often make no attempt to clean the site of the radioactive waste contaminating the land. These sites are unusuable. Cleaning up and removing the waste is the only way they can be speedily restored to a safe condition and used again for other purposes.

Waste can be stored underground. Plans are already under way in the USA to store waste left over from making nuclear weapons. But no decision has yet been made about what to do with nuclear power station waste. In most cases the power stations are storing their waste on the station site. It will remain there until decisions are made about what to do with it. The trouble is that it is being stored close to centres of population.

CASE STUDY

The Chernobyl accident occurred when one of the station's reactors melted down and exploded, blasting radiation dust into the air. Rain then washed some of it back down on to the surrounding land. Winds also blew some of it across Russia into the atmosphere over other countries in northern Europe, where it fell on to the land and contaminated animals and plants. Many of the thousands who were involved in the clean up at Chernobyl died of radioactive poisoning and many in the surrounding area suffered radioactive burns from the **fallout**. It is estimated that nearly 30,000 will eventually die of cancer because of radioactive contamination.

MARALINGA

On the Aboriginal land of Maralinga in the desert of South Australia hundreds of square kilometres were designated for testing British nuclear weapons in the 1950s. The land became so contaminated that it still isn't fit for humans to live in. The Aborigines will wait a long time before they can return to their land.

RADIOACTIVE BIRDS

In 1999 seagulls and pigeons in the vicinity of the Sellafield nuclear power station in north-west England were found to be contaminated by radioactive pollution. The seagulls' droppings were radioactive and the pigeons had been contaminated after roosting in old buildings on the nuclear station site.

Making the nuclear world safer

It is clear to most of us that **nuclear** weapons and waste have the potential to cause devastation to people and the environment. So, it is vital something is done to protect the world from the dangers. Nuclear power stations need to be made safer, nuclear weapons sites have to be cleaned up and nuclear waste has to be safely stored. Also we have to get rid of more nuclear weapons and stop building them altogether. If you live near a nuclear power station or weapons-making factory, you will be particularly concerned about how nuclear waste is being stored and what the risks of a nuclear accident are.

Making nuclear power stations safer

Nuclear power stations in western countries have been redesigned to make them safer. A reactor now has a safety device that automatically shuts off the reactor if it gets too hot, in this way avoiding an explosion. Also the cores of reactors are encased in a concrete and steel structure so that they do not release radiation into the atmosphere if there is **meltdown** and an explosion.

After the Three Mile Island incident the nuclear industry in America set up the Institute of Nuclear Power Operations (INPO). The purpose was to get different power stations to discuss safety with one another and to pass on technical information that would help to improve safety.

Cleaning up the land

Sites contaminated by **radioactive** waste can be cleaned up and made safe to use again. But to clean up all the contaminated land will take a long time and cost a massive amount of money. The Americans think it will take them about 75 years to clean up all their contaminated land and it will cost at least $200 billion.

Storing waste

The problem of storing the waste raises doubts about whether the nuclear power industry can survive or go on progressing. If we can't sort out the way we handle the waste then perhaps we need to look at shifting to alternative energy sources. This is already happening in Sweden where the government has decided to phase out nuclear power and replace it with other energy sources.

CASE STUDY

Hanford in north-west USA once had a busy nuclear weapons industry, with a factory standing on the banks of the Columbia river. From here nuclear waste was dumped into the river and the surrounding soil, making it a highly contaminated site. However, by 1995 it had been cleaned up and turned into a recreational and wildlife park. Radiation levels in the area have returned to normal.

In the mid-1990s Greenpeace was directly involved in trying to stop the French carrying out atmospheric tests in the Pacific.

Nuclear test bans

People have protested against nuclear weapons since the early days of atmospheric testing in the 1950s. The protest movement spread during the 1950s and 1960s, the most notable group being CND (Campaign for Nuclear Disarmament), which organized the annual Easter protest march to the Aldermarston nuclear research station in Berkshire in southern England. Marches and demonstrations were also held in London, sometimes erupting into disturbances that ended with demonstrators being arrested. The movement against nuclear weapons is still active and relevant, particularly in view of the recent nuclear developments in India and Pakistan.

The impact of early opposition to nuclear weapons on world leaders may have influenced the leaders of America, Britain and the Soviet Union to reach agreement in 1963 to cease nuclear testing in the atmosphere. These powers signed the Limited Test Ban Treaty, under which they agreed to carry out nuclear testing underground from then on.

A succession of other treaties between the nuclear powers followed over the years. Each of them reduced or banned the production of a range of weapons. When the START II treaty was signed in 1993 it was the first time that the superpowers had agreed to get rid of more weapons than they were making.

WHAT YOU CAN DO

- Join a campaign against storing of nuclear waste in power stations in your locality.
- Join environmental groups who are opposed to nuclear testing and the storing of nuclear waste.
- Help fund-raising for protest movements.

The price of using energy

Do you enjoy the winter warmth and comfort of your home and the convenience of having hot water on tap whenever you want? This is only possible by using energy. Electricity or gas is used to heat the water that flows through your central heating system and from your bathroom tap. You may also appreciate the convenience and speed of being taken to school in a car. This also is only possible by generating energy, and this is done by burning fuel or petrol.

These comforts and conveniences however have a price. The gases given off by the generation of energy to propel cars and aeroplanes and to heat houses and water pass into the atmosphere where they build up and cause serious air **pollution**. You are then affected by having to breathe contaminated air, which can damage your health. Poor air also damages the health of plants and animals. The extraction (removal) of the resources – coal, oil, natural gas, uranium – needed to generate energy involves damaging landscapes and polluting soils. Oil and natural gas pipelines stretch across huge areas of wilderness land and disturb the wildlife that inhabits those areas.

Fossil fuel

The main **fossil fuels** are coal, oil and natural gas. These are extracted from the earth. The extraction and use of them affects the health and lives of people, animals and plants.

Coal

Extracting coal changes a landscape. Mining coal involves boring and digging deep holes and long tunnels under the earth or excavating huge areas on the surface. Underground mining leaves behind coal waste piled high in **slag heaps** that blot the landscape. **Opencast** mining changes the landscape by blowing out the sides of hills with explosives and gouging out rock and soil with huge earth-moving machinery.

If you live in the vicinity of such workings you cannot help being affected by them. Poisonous materials in the slag heaps are often washed out of the heaps and seep into the underground water, which is often used as drinking water, and into rivers. This poisons the fish in the rivers and if humans are fishing for food the poison enters the human food chain through people consuming the fish.

CASE STUDY

Slag heaps are also dangerous in other ways. In the coal-mining village of Aberfan in Wales in 1966, a huge slag heap saturated with rainwater became unstable and moved down the side of the valley and buried the village primary school that stood in its path. Of the 144 people killed, 116 were children.

Burning coal gives off sulphur dioxide, one of the gases that cause acid rain. This can kill trees, destroy fertile soil and damage buildings. The gases given off by coal-burning are also sources of the main **greenhouse gases** and contribute to **global warming**.

Oil and natural gas

Oil is used as a fuel for motor vehicles and aeroplanes, for heating, and as bitumen for road surfaces. As a fossil fuel it adds to greenhouse gases in the atmosphere and to acid rain through **emissions** by motor vehicles and aeroplanes. The biggest consumers are the industrialized countries of the West: the USA uses 25 per cent of the world's supply and Europe over half.

Natural gas is cleaner than coal and oil and used by those seeking to reduce air pollution. However it does add to greenhouse gases. This tends to come from leaking pipelines, oil/gas wells and domestic use. Pipelines can rupture causing oil to spill out on to the land. This will happen if the pipelines are not maintained or deteriorate through age.

Nuclear energy

Some argue that nuclear energy is cleaner than other energies. However it needs uranium which is mined using the opencast method. This leaves massive scars on the landscape, poisonous waste and damages the lives of indigenous people in the areas where it is mined.

CASE STUDY

The Mirrar Aboriginal tribe of northern Australia in 1999 opposed the Energy Resources of Australia company's right to mine the uranium on their land (at Jabiluka in the Northern Territory). They believed that this will lead, not only to over 80 hectares of land being stripped, but the left-over toxic (poisonous) wastes being buried within the Kakadu National Park, a protected wildlife area.

Hydroelectric energy

Hydroelectricity is clean energy but it does cause serious environmental and human problems. Dams and reservoirs need to be built and this means clearing land of its natural cover – trees and plants – and disturbing the habitats of animals and the lives of the people who live and work in the area affected. Dams can also fracture and flood the land below, wiping out people and their farms and homes.

Uranium is needed for nuclear energy but mining causes damage to the landscape and also to the health of indigenous people.

Using cleaner energy

We are using more energy every year. The big challenge is to come up with ways that enable us to make better use of the energy resources of the country, to find new sources of energy and to prevent damaging the environment. We all need electricity: to light our homes, power our computers and boil our kettles. However we have a choice as to where we get our electricity from. New, more environmentally-friendly ways of generating electricity are being developed and we could choose to take our electricity from these, in some cases now and more so in the future when they become more commercially developed.

Renewable energy

Renewable energy resources are cleaner than **fossil fuels**, give out less **greenhouse gases** and do not add to acid rain. Also because oil and natural gas resources will diminish in the next century it is crucial to look for alternatives. Here are some of these.

Hydroelectric energy

This is the use of water power to generate electricity. It's used throughout the world and is the world's main renewable energy resource. Its potential is said to be twice what is presently being produced.

Tidal and wave energy

There are possibilities for the use of tidal and wave power to generate electricity, though this is still at the experimental stage in many cases. In Britain there are tidal schemes for the Severn, Mersey, Wye, Conway and Humber estuaries.

Solar energy

The heat of the Sun is being used to generate electricity in many countries, especially those with lots of sun. The Kramer Junction power farm in California's Mojave Desert has 600,000 mirrors pointing at the Sun to capture the heat from its rays. This farm produces most of the world's usable solar energy. Even in Britain, with its more limited hours of sunshine, solar energy is being used, especially for heating houses specially designed to generate solar energy.

Geothermal energy

This generates electricity from the heat of rocks and hot underground water. Several countries use it as a source of energy. California in particular produces more than 2000 megawatts. In Britain hot salt waters under Southampton are tapped to heat buildings.

Wind power

The use of wind to generate electricity. Wind farms are expensive to set up but cheap to run. Some countries are much keener on this than others. Holland planned to have 2000 windmills by the end of the twentieth century and Denmark was planning to draw 10 per cent of its energy from **wind power** by the same time. Britain has by far the greatest wind power potential in Europe, however it has failed to take more advantage of this.

Biomass energy

This is the use of animal and plant waste to generate electricity. It works by using

An energy-efficient building in Amsterdam which has solar panels plus modern insulation to help store heat.

the waste of a **landfill** site which breaks down naturally and releases energy – methane gas. This provides up to 14 per cent of the world's energy. In Britain the first wood-fired biomass power station started operating in 1999 in Yorkshire, producing gas with only small amounts of sulphur emissions.

Government action

Governments can direct the use of alternative energy sources rather than fossil fuel. The Non-Fossil Fuel Obligation in Britain is one programme in which regional electricity-generating companies have to provide customers with part of their electricity from **nuclear** and renewable sources. Some countries impose levies on fossil-fuel generating electricity and use the money raised to spend on electricity using non-fossil fuel, as in the case of the UK Fossil Fuel Levy.

Energy efficiency

Buildings can be made more energy efficient. They can be better insulated, better designed to allow in more natural light and draw their heat and electricity from the same source. Houses can be built to face south and east to capture more of the Sun's light and heat.

Incentives can be offered to encourage people to make more use of public transport. Motor engines could be better designed and unleaded petrol could be used more. Electric cars and trams can be used in city centres to cut down fossil-fuel pollution and noise. The tram is a familiar sight in some European cities, such as Amsterdam and Geneva, and in British cities, such as Sheffield in Yorkshire.

Another way of shifting the high-level use of energy (electricity) is for electricity-supply companies to offer a range of products that conserve energy and make homes more efficient, such as thermal insulation and energy efficient light bulbs.

WHAT YOU CAN DO

- Save energy by turning off the lights whenever you leave a room.
- Shut doors and windows to cut down draughts and noise

The hazards of waste

We need coal to generate electricity, oil to run our motor cars, uranium to make **nuclear** fuel, and so on. In extracting these from the earth we leave behind what we do not need. This is the waste. In the case of mining uranium it will be rocks and soil laced with poisonous chemicals, in the case of factories making pharmaceuticals it will include chemical detergents, and in the case of nuclear power stations it will include **radioactive** fuel rods. In buying and consuming/using food, clothes, newspapers, magazines, and so on, we discard what we do not want or no longer want. This includes packaging – wrapping paper, cartons, bottles – unwanted food, old clothes, newspapers and magazines we have finished reading. We also produce household waste that we dispose of through the **sewage** system.

Household waste

You probably have some idea of how much food your family buys in a week. You can see from looking at the supermarket trolley how much of it is packaged in cartons, bottles and cans. You then consume the food during the week and dispose of any uneaten food and unwanted packaging, bottles and cans in the rubbish bin. Your rubbish is collected once a week by a rubbish disposal company, which takes it to a **landfill** site for dumping. The site is created by digging holes in the ground and this is filled in by dumping household rubbish in it.

Rubbish and waste is dumped at landfill sites like this one in Dundee, Scotland.

Toilet waste is disposed of through the sewage system and dumped in rivers and the sea – sometimes after treatment, sometimes untreated. Untreated toilet waste can poison life in rivers, as happened in the case of London, which at one time became so contaminated by sewage and industrial waste that nothing could survive in it. The river was eventually declared to be 'dead'.

> **FACT**
>
> ● *Each British household creates 1 tonne of waste a year. In all 450 million tonnes of waste is produced in Britain every year.*

Mining waste

Most industries rely on natural minerals that have to be taken out of the ground. But when we mine minerals from the ground we leave behind what we don't want – usually rocks and soil which may contain dangerous chemicals. In uranium mining, for example, we leave behind a poisonous chemical called radium and in copper mining we leave behind arsenic and cadmium. Rain may then wash these into rivers and lakes and they could also seep into **groundwater** and enter drinking water supplies. The contaminated water may be a cause of bone cancer. This happened in the case of the Ok Tedi copper mine in Papua New Guinea.

Industrial waste

Industries such as the chemical industry leave behind poisonous waste from the production of their goods. Industrial companies often get rid of their waste by dumping it on the land or into rivers, lakes and seas.

Nuclear waste

The nuclear test bans of the 1970s and 1980s and the reductions in making nuclear weapons meant that many weapons-making factories had to close down. When this happened they left behind land that was badly contaminated by the chemical waste of the factories. In the case of Rocky Mountain in Denver, USA, where weapons, including nerve gas, were made, the land had become so contaminated that it was impossible for people and wildlife to live there.

Nuclear waste from power stations is presently still piling up in some parts of the world waiting to be moved to permanent storage sites. In the meantime it's being stored on site at the power stations. Some of it is stored in the station itself in water-cooled pools and some of it in the grounds of the station in steel and concrete casks. A danger is that casks might leak radioactivity into the air. Another problem is that some of these power stations are close to sizeable towns and any accident and leaking of radioactive waste would endanger the people living there.

CASE STUDY

One of the most notorious cases of waste dumping was that of Love Canal in Niagara Falls in New York state. In the early 1950s a new community was built on the site of a former dumping ground for the waste of a chemical-making factory owned by the Hooker Chemical Corporation. In time poisonous chemicals started seeping from the soil into the houses and is believed to have caused various health problems among the people living there, such as cancer, birth defects and low birth weights.

Handling waste

Humans produce millions of tonnes of waste every year. We need to have ways of storing it, destroying it, or recycling it. Whether it is household waste or industrial waste it has to be disposed of safely so it does not harm us and the environment. If we have to dump it in **landfill** sites then these have to be properly managed to make sure the waste does not in time turn poisonous and leak out into the environment and contaminate us. If we are dumping it in our rivers and seas then it should be properly treated so that it cannot poison the life of the seas and rivers, and in time us. If we **incinerate** the waste we should be sure that the **emissions** are harmless to us and the environment.

Storing the waste

Waste can be disposed of by being stored in a special site or by burning. There are various ways this can be done.

Landfills

You are more familiar with landfill sites used for dumping household rubbish. Perhaps there is one near where you live. If you have seen one, you will have noticed the amount of rubbish being dumped in them. These tend to be left uncovered. The rubbish is allowed to break down naturally.

Toxic waste needs to be more carefully stored. The most common way is to dump it in a special landfill site. This is a hole in the ground that is filled up and then covered with clay. Regular inspections are made and the site is landscaped.

Britain has about 4000 landfill sites and most are well managed, with very few leaking any toxic waste.

Underground storage

We tend to be most concerned about what to do with **nuclear** waste. This waste has been dumped in the sea in the past and is still going on. Nuclear waste can also be stored underground where the rocks are stable, where there is little rain to wash away leaking waste and where there are very few people. These conditions are why Carlsbad in the New Mexico desert was chosen to store some of America's nuclear waste.

Dry cask storage

Spent nuclear rods are stored in steel and concrete casks in the grounds of a nuclear power station. But there are worries about the risk of casks rupturing and leaking **radioactive** waste, particularly in sites close to towns. The US government is committed to moving all the nuclear waste stored in sites throughout the country to specially designated safe sites far from centres of population.

Burning the waste

Waste can be burned in huge incinerators. One of the advantages of incineration is that it's a way of recycling toxic waste. Some of it can be burned in cement factory kilns to produce energy for the kilns. Chemical weapons, such as nerve gas, can also be burned. In Britain toxic waste incinerators are said to be safe. The trouble is that people just don't like having waste incinerators in their neighbourhood. In 1992 in Jacksonville, Arkansas, locals protested at the proposal to install a toxic waste incinerator in the city, and residents of the Bronx in New York made it clear they were absolutely against the plan for a local incinerator to burn hospital waste.

Recycling waste

Much of our household waste can be recycled. In your local area you will find collection points, recycling and waste reception centres. Here you can dispose of bottles, cans, newspapers and clothes. Some city councils may also have a collection service for newspapers, cans, foil and clothes.

PAYING FOR THE CLEAN UP

Given that we have a case of **pollution** we then need to clean it up and dispose of it safely. But this is expensive, so who pays? Obviously whoever caused the pollution. There are two ways this can be done.

Polluter-pays principle
In the USA and Europe there are laws to force a polluter to pay the cost of cleaning up the pollution they are responsible for. In the UK the Environmental Protection Act of 1992 forces operators of open landfill sites who have caused pollution to pay to clean it up.

Taxing the polluter
In the USA in 1980 a Superfund was set up to pay for any contamination of land. The cost of this was raised from taxes imposed on companies: a petroleum tax, a corporate environment tax, a tax on chemical feedstock, as well as money from general taxation.

GREEN TAX

Europeans are proposing to introduce a 'green' tax that would be imposed on potential polluters to cover any clean up needed in the future. However, some countries may be stricter than others in imposing the tax.

A Greenpeace demonstration.

The hazards of nature

Our lives are affected by nature in varying ways and to different degrees. You have probably seen on TV some of the recent natural disasters of the world. Nature at its most powerful can cause havoc and destruction in the human world. In 1998 there were 700 major natural disasters in the world. In that year 50,000 people died and 300 million were made homeless as a result.

Fire

Fire can be caused by nature or humans. Natural fires can start from spontaneous combustion, or, more commonly, from lightning, which strikes the surface of the planet 100,000 times a day.

Fire can wipe out vast areas of forest in a short time. The loss of trees and plants exposes soil to leaching, loss of nutrients, erosion and destroys the cooling shade that trees provide. Out of control bush fires can destroy homes and plants and kill animals and humans.

Flood

Every year in various parts of the world rivers overflow, killing people and damaging farming land. Floods are caused by high rains, melting snow and breached dams. Heavily populated low-lying areas on river floodplains are particularly vulnerable to flooding, as in the Ganges-Brahmaputra-Megna basin on the Indian subcontinent.

Drought

Millions of people and animals and vast areas of crops can die from drought in the poorer parts of the world. Drought occurs after a long period without enough rain for growing crops. This can happen anywhere, but most disastrously in those areas of the world where people depend on **subsistence** agriculture to survive.

Earthquake

A serious earthquake can cause massive natural and human damage: landslides, giant waves (tsunamis), fires, flooding, collapse of buildings and roads, and

The Turkish earthquake in 1999 occurred along a known fault line through the country's most populated industrialized region.

death. The scale of human disaster will depend on how many people are concentrated in the vicinity and how well they have prepared themselves against natural hazards. The first earthquake that struck Turkey in 1999 demolished thousands of poorly constructed buildings and killed 45,000 people.

Tornadoes, cyclones and thunderstorms

Tornadoes are powerful wind storms with spinning columns of air that move at speeds in excess of 115km/hr. In the short time a tornado lasts it can do monstrous damage, making it one of the most feared natural hazards. It can tear trees out of the ground by their roots, wreck houses and office blocks and toss cars hundreds of metres away. It can even cause deaths.

Tropical cyclones or hurricanes can blow at 300km/hr, strong enough to kill people and destroy property. Six thousand people died in Galveston, Texas, in 1900 when a hurricane ripped through the coastal city, the worst hurricane disaster in American history.

Thunderstorms are torrential rain, hailstorms and lightning. About 2000 are going on at any one time throughout the world. Hailstorms can damage crops, houses and cars, and lightning can kill people, with an average of five being killed in Britain every year and about 95 in the USA.

WHAT CAN BE DONE

● **Preventing disaster**
The effect of drought can be avoided to some extent by changing traditional subsistence farming methods that exhaust the soil of its **nutrients**. Rotating the crops every so often, fertilising the soil, conserving rainwater and using irrigation where possible will protect the soil from becoming exhausted and useless for growing food.

Dams can be built to hold water for drinking and irrigation. In India there is less risk of drought because of the Tabela Dam. In poor, arid countries there are international aid programmes for tapping underground aquifers to draw up water clean enough for drinking.

● **Warnings of disaster**
Predicting natural disaster is possible. People who are most in danger can then be warned to protect themselves.

The chance of a river flooding can be calculated using stream gauges to keep a watch on a river's water height. At the critical point warnings would then be sent out to the people in the flood area.

Tornadoes are difficult to predict. However in 'Tornado Valley' (in Oklahoma) in the USA there is a tornado watch system that keeps people in touch with tornado movement through radio and TV reports. Weather satellites can be used to predict when cyclones will occur and warnings are then sent out to those living in the coastal regions likely to be hit.

● **Minimising disaster**
Much of the death and destruction caused by earthquakes involve buildings. Buildings that cannot withstand the shocks created by an earthquake will crumble and collapse, killing people in and around them. One idea for preventing buildings collapsing is to fit massive ball bearings under them. The bearings will move as the earth moves during an earthquake, preventing the buildings cracking and collapsing.

What can I do?

Like many people you may feel that whatever you do as an individual makes no difference in the greater scheme of things. Charity organizations such as Oxfam realized that this was a problem when they were making their appeals for help. People couldn't see what difference their contribution would make to the millions of people who were starving throughout the world. Oxfam realized they had to make their appeal, not as if they were asking people to help solve the whole problem, but as if they were asking them to help a single child or a single family. In this way people could see how they could make a difference.

Preserving the environment and repairing some of the damage that has been done can be viewed in a similar way. As individuals we cannot solve the whole problem, but we can each play a part. Consider what you have the power to do in your everyday life to prevent further damage and to repair the current damage.

CHANGING YOUR EATING HABITS

- If you feel strongly about farmers using artificial chemicals, you can try to eat as much **organically** grown food as possible – i.e. food grown with the use of natural **fertilizers** which do not contaminate the environment.
- You might also decide not to eat food produced by factory farms because of the **effluent** that washes from these farms into rivers.
- You could change to eating free range eggs and change to eating meat from free-range cattle or pigs.

If retailers perceive a change in consumer buying to organic and free-range foods they may put pressure on farmers to change their ways of farming. The pressure would then be on governments to support organic farmers more, so increasing the range of organic produce and bringing the costs down for the consumer.

ASK QUESTIONS

- If your drinking water tastes horrible you can report this to the water company or the Environment Agency and ask them to let you know why this has happened.

- If you suffer from asthma or some other chest complaint that makes breathing difficult in polluted air, you can phone the government's air pollution service (0800 55 66 77) for reports on how bad air pollution levels are on particular days.

REDUCE POLLUTION

- Reduce **emissions** by avoiding aerosol sprays and using alternatives.
- Reduce emissions by using as little heating as you can. Central heating gives off gases into the atmosphere. The level of heating can be reduced when you go to bed at night and can be timed to shut down during the day when there is no one in the house.
- Persuade your family to help reduce water pollution by using washing powders and washing-up liquids that are free of **phosphates** and are biodegradable.

SAVE ENERGY

- Save energy by turning off the lights at night, switching off the TV completely – do not leave it on stand-by – and switching off the computer.
- Close doors to hold in the warmth.
- Save energy by using less electrical equipment in the home – e.g. food mixers, electric screwdrivers.
- Save water by having a shower instead of a bath.

REPORTING POLLUTION

- If you spot oil **pollution** on your local beach (usually this comes from an oil tanker moored off the coast washing the remnants of oil out of its bilges after unloading its oil cargo in port), report it quickly to the authorities. It might be possible to locate the culprit tanker and impose fines or take action against the owners.

RECYCLE

- Start a compost heap or a compost bucket by collecting organic waste (e.g. vegetable peelings and uncooked food). This can be recycled as garden fertilizer.
- Try and recycle glass, cans, paper, plastic and clothes. Deposit non-returnable bottles and jars in the nearest bottle bank – wash them out first. Take your cans to the nearest can collection point and again wash these out and squash them so they are ready for recycling. Larger pieces of metal can be taken to scrap metal dealers. Newspapers and other waste paper can be recycled. Bundle and tie them up for collection or take them to your nearest recycling centre.

Very few of us escape pollution yet we all want to live in a pleasant and rubbish-free environment. It's worth picking up litter, putting back a shopping trolley and recycling that aluminium can…

Glossary

algae water plants, including seaweed. They become poisonous when they decay.

bacteria known as germs, these cause human disease and are found in air, soil, water and other animals

birth control limiting the number of children born

catalytic converters device used as part of motor vehicle exhaust system for changing harmful gases into less harmful ones

CFCs (chlorofluorocarbons) gases used in aerosol cans, refrigerators, air conditioners and in making foam boxes for holding fast food

conservation the steps taken to protect and preserve the Earth's natural resources

contaminate to pollute air, land and water with waste and poisonous substances

contraceptives devices or ways of preventing pregnancy

corrosive the eating away of material by chemicals

ecosystem the way living things exist together in a specific place, e.g ponds

effluent liquid waste

emissions the sending out of gases into the atmosphere

European Community a community of European countries working together

Everglades a swampy, subtropical area in Florida in the USA

fallout the radioactive dust that falls back to earth after a nuclear explosion

fertilizers chemicals used in farming and gardening to add more nutrients to the soil to improve the growth of plants and crops

food chain the order in which living things feed on other living things

fossil fuel fuel such as coal and oil that has been formed from the fossil remains of animals and plants

global warming the rise in the world's temperature due to greenhouse gases

green belt area areas set aside to be free of urban development. The aim is to stop cities expanding into the countryside.

greenhouse effect gases in the atmosphere stop heat returning from the Earth to space. Air pollution has increased the amount of these gases and this is thought to be a cause of global warming.

greenhouse gases include carbon dioxide, methane, nitrous oxides and water vapour. They form a layer in the stratosphere (the lower level of the atmosphere).

groundwater fresh water that has gathered in rocks underground and which can be drawn to the surface and used as drinking water

hydrofluorocarbons (HFCs) these belong to the same group of chemicals as CFCs

incinerate to burn, as in the case of burning waste, particularly radioactive waste

indigenous native people

insecticide chemicals used to kill insects

intensive farming producing as much from the land as possible by using fertilizers and spraying crops

landfill a site in which a huge hole is dug in the ground and filled up with waste

leaching the washing out of nutrients in the soil

meltdown when the core of the reactor in a nuclear power station reaches melting point the fuel rods start melting. Radioactive material might then be released into the atmosphere.

nitrates fertilizers used in farming

nutrients parts of food such as carbohydrates, protein, fat, minerals, vitamins

organic a way of farming that uses natural fertilizers (e.g manure) to improve the soil

ozone a gas that forms in the upper layer of the atmosphere. In the lower layers of the atmosphere it is a pollutant that contributes to greenhouse gases. At ground level it can trigger asthma attacks. It also contributes to smog.

ozone layer the layer of ozone gas that protects the earth from the harmful ultraviolet rays of the Sun

pesticides chemicals used to kill pests, such as insects, weeds and other things that harm plants

phosphates fertilizers used for helping the growth of plants

pollution substances such as gases that get into the environment and cause it harm

radioactivity consists of particles and radiation waves

rainforest forest found in tropical areas. They have a huge range of animal and plant life.

reactor a device for producing nuclear energy

respiratory disease an illness which makes breathing difficult

runoff the flow of rainwater over land

saturated full of liquid

sewage human waste from households, factories and street drains

slag heaps large mounds of waste, such as coal waste, left behind during the mining of minerals from the earth

smog a haze caused by pollutants in the air. It is a mixture of gases and it can cause breathing problems for people.

solvent used for dissolving something

subsistence agriculture a way of farming in which people use only what is available from the land

sustainable to maintain the sources of materials such as wood by renewing, reusing and recycling them

ultraviolet a form of radiation (as in sunlight)

United Nations an organization of the world's nations with the aims of peace, security and cooperation

World Health Organization part of the United Nations, it was set up to prevent the spread of diseases and to get rid of them

Contacts and helplines

AIR POLLUTION SERVICE
0800 55 66 77
www.environment.detr.gov.uk/airq

COUNTRYSIDE COMMISSION
John Dower House, Crescent Place
Cheltenham, Gloucestershire, GL50 3RA
01242 521381

COUNTRYSIDE COUNCIL FOR WALES
Plas Penrhos, Ffordd Penrhos, Bangor,
Gwynedd, LL57 2LQ
01248 385500
www.ccw.gov.uk

DRINKING WATER INSPECTORATE
Floor 2/A1 Ashdown House
123 Victoria Street, London, SW1E 6DE
020 7890 5956
www.dwi.detr.gov.uk

ENGLISH NATURE
Northminster House, Peterborough
PE1 1UA
01733 455100

ENVIRONMENT AGENCY
Rio House, Waterside Drive, Aztec West
Almondsbury, Bristol, BS32 4UD
0645 333 111
www.environment-agency.gov.uk
Report any environmental problems
affecting the air, land and water by calling
the Agency hotline on *0800 80 70 60*

FRIENDS OF THE EARTH
26-28 Underwood Street, London, N1 7JQ
020 7490 1555

GREENPEACE
Canonbury Villas, London, N1 2PN
020 7865 8100
www.greenpeace.org.uk
www.greenpeace.org.uk/greenbytes is a
site especially for young people

MARINE CONSERVATION SOCIETY
9 Gloucester Road, Ross-on-Wye
Herefordshire, HR9 5BU
01989 566017
www.mcsuk.mcmail.com

NATIONAL TRUST
36 Queen Anne's Gate
London, SW1H 9AS
020 7222 9251

SCOTTISH NATURAL HERITAGE
www.snh.org.uk

ULSTER WILDLIFE TRUST
Ulster Wildlife Centre
3 New Line, Crossgar
Co Down
N. Ireland
028 4483 0282

WORLD WILDLIFE FUND
Panda House, Weyside Park, Godalming
Surrey, GU7 1XR
0483 426 444

IN AUSTRALIA

ENVIRONMENT PROTECTION AUTHORITY
www.epa.vic.gov.au (Victoria)
www.epa.nsw.gov.au (New South Wales)

EPA POLLUTION WATCH LINE
(03) 9695 2777 (Victoria)
13 1555 (New South Wales)

**GREENPEACE AUSTRALIA –
PACIFIC**
Level 4, 35-39 Liverpool Street
Sydney, NSW 2000
2 9261 4666
greenpeace@au.greenpeace.org

Further reading

Non-fiction

New Modular Science: Environment
Heinemann 1997

Examining Environmental Issues
Sue Penney
Heinemann 1993

Friends of the Earth
Free booklets on:

*Don't Burn It or Buy It: Alternatives to
Landfills and Incinerators*

Disappearing Forest

Energy and the Environment

The Green Energy Guide

Our Threatened Wildlife

Poisoning Our Children

Road Transport and Air Pollution

Waste

Water Pollution

**Other publications by
Friends of the Earth:**

Don't Throw It Away

Energy Without End

Index